*To profit from good advice requires more wisdom
than to give it.*

John Churton

—————————————

onprofit organizations are increasingly turning to advisory boards for help. These advisory bodies, also called advisory committees, councils, or task forces, are often expected to assist the nonprofit's staff and governing board in fund-raising and friend-raising activities. In some cases, they are asked to provide professional expertise to strengthen a specific program.

An advisory committee is a voluntary group of individuals assembled to advise or support an organization (or one of its programs). Unlike the members of a governing board who serve as fiduciaries and policymakers, the members of an advisory committee are not typically authorized to act as decisionmakers. Generally, the advisory committee's authority is limited to giving advice and counsel to the governing board, the executive director or chief staff officer, or other members of the staff.

A successful advisory group can do much to help an organization fulfill its mission. Advisory board members have helped enormously in raising funds, addressing political problems, handling public relations, and reviewing programs. An unsuccessful advisory group, on the other hand, can be a costly drain on precious institutional resources, image, and good will. Much of the advisory group's success rests upon the chief executive officer assigned responsibility for engaging it.

This booklet has been prepared for those who work with or serve on advisory boards, and is written in response to the many inquiries directed to the author by executive directors and board members who are either contemplating the creation of a new advisory structure, or deciding whether to restructure an ineffective one (see Appendix A for questions to consider in advance).

I. PURPOSES OF ADVISORY COMMITTEES

Advisory groups are established to serve many functions including:

♦ Raising money for unrestricted use or for a specific program;

♦ Serving as advocates for the organization to the community it serves;

♦ Providing feedback to the organization from the community;

♦ Reviewing, monitoring, or assessing a specific program;

♦ Evaluating the performance of the organization;

♦ Providing a means for involving people who are willing to give very critical assistance, but have limited time (this category might include a highly placed public official, an influential business person, or someone with access to potential large donors);

♦ Providing technical expertise;

♦ Gathering input from or serving as a liaison with relevant constituencies;

♦ Building a corp of outside, experienced experts whose interest and support are important (including possible future board members or former board members who can continue to make a contribution to the organization); and

♦ Providing an independent, unbiased sounding board.

Some advisory groups are mandated by the organization's financial supporters to provide a kind of "public check" on the funds that are appropriated. Many nonprofit organizations have been successful in expanding the role of these "required" groups from performing exclusively for the benefit of funders or regulators to a mechanism that contributes broadly to management and governance.

Some advisory committees are permanent bodies, while others have a limited term of existence. It is important for the organization to fix the period of existence of this group, if this is known in advance. Sometimes, an organization will create an advisory committee as an ad hoc group to address a specific issue such as a capital campaign. In other cases, a new program might begin with an advisory committee before evolving into an independent entity with its own governing board.

The legal liability of the members of the advisory committee must also be assessed. Although the members of an advisory group are not generally exposed to the same degree of liability as the members of the governing board, the advisors should be protected by the nonprofit organization's risk management policies (including adequate insurance coverage), if appropriate.

II. INGREDIENTS FOR A SUCCESSFUL ADVISORY COMMITTEE

The universe of advisory committee structures reflects the remarkable diversity of nonprofit organizations in the United States. One size does not fit all. A variety of advisory committee roles and structures have been successfully tailored to fit the different kinds of organizations they serve. Many variables influence the role as well as the effectiveness of the advisory committee such as: the governance and management structure of the organization it advises; the group authorized to select its members; its specific purpose and composition; its developmental stage and authorized life span; the budget and staff that support it; and, perhaps most important, the leadership style of both staff and committee leaders.

Given this diversity, it is difficult to generalize and impossible to dispense neat formulas for success. A "successful" advisory committee is defined here as fulfilling the purpose for which it was established. An advisory committee is relatively easy to establish. Although many advisory committees have made substantial contributions to the organizations they serve, a growing gap between expectations and performance has led to dissatisfaction among many who serve on or work with these groups. Appendix B identifies some of the common problems with advisory committees.

The following case studies are composites of actual examples. Although too brief and too incomplete to be followed by customized prescriptions, these cases identify some of the most common contributions and frustrations associated with advisory groups. They also illustrate the qualities and characteristics that seem to make some advisory committees work so much better than others.

The reader is cautioned to heed H.L. Mencken's warning, "For every complicated problem, there is a solution that is simple, elegant . . . and wrong." Any diagnosis of a dysfunctional advisory committee needs to distinguish symptoms from underlying causes. Much of this responsibility will ultimately fall on the executive director or senior administrator who is charged with staffing the advisory committee.

III. CASE #1: A Clearly Defined Purpose

> *When John Keaton becomes the new executive director of the Genetic Diseases National Health Agency (GDNHA), he begins to question the existence of the advisory committee. No one on the governing board, the staff, or the advisory committee has been able to give him a sense of what the group has accomplished. Hired with a major mandate to get rid of the deficit and raise more funds, John is concerned about the costs of bringing together members of the advisory committee who come from different regions of the country for a dinner twice a year. When he brings this to the attention of his board chairperson, she assures him that GDNHA should maintain this "group of prominent people because of their fund-raising potential—and let's face it—our current governing board isn't going to be able to raise the dollars that we need."*

Advisory bodies can attract distinguished, high-level people who bring invaluable contacts, visibility, and support. Far too many advisory committees are formed, however, only because it seems like a good idea or because it has great potential. The fervor with which these committees are established can ebb quickly. To counter this possibility, the organization should identify the specific purpose of the advisory group before establishing or renewing it.

GDNHA's advisory committee seems to have been formed for fund-raising purposes, but little evidence suggests that the members are aware of that purpose or that they have been successful. This sounds like a good time for the governing board and the new executive director to revisit the role of this group by restating explicitly the reason for its existence. If the purpose is fund raising, what is the difference between the fund-raising roles of the governing board and the advisory committee? If GDNHA cannot channel adequate resources into helping this committee raise funds (or if the resources are not generating adequate results), it may decide to add more people to the governing board who can help with fund raising. At this stage in GDNHA's life cycle, the board and Keaton may also consider reorganizing the advisory committee to serve another important purpose for the agency, such as providing medical advice on research or patient care, or providing advice on how to improve relations with local chapters.

Advisory committees are dynamic – their role will shift as circumstances change. Therefore it is important not only to make the initial purpose as explicit as possible, but also to review the purpose as well as the performance of the group on a regular basis. Advisory committees work most effectively when they can focus on a specific task or component within the organization. The greater the clarity of purpose, the more explicit can be the responsibilities of individual members.

When establishing an advisory committee for fund-raising purposes, it is important to determine whether this effort supplements the work of the governing board or consists of a full delegation of one of the governing board's responsibilities. It is unrealistic to expect the advisory committee to do something that board members want to avoid. On the other hand, it is not unreasonable to ask such a group to *assist* the board and staff in this important activity.

IV. CASE #2: A Written Statement of Organization and Purpose

Cynthia Wu, the executive director, and Martin Chamberlain, the advisory committee president, agree that the advisory committee's major purpose is to help enhance the Falstaff Performing Arts Center's position in the community it serves. The Center has never been able to recruit managers from local corporations to serve on its advisory committee. When Cynthia and Martin call on the executive vice president of their local retail chain to serve on their committee, he is reluctant to join because of other commitments. He is a strong supporter of the Center, but he can't seem to get from Cynthia and Martin a clear sense of the specific role of the group and what he will be expected to do as an individual committee member.

A written statement of organization and purpose helps an advisory committee to identify the entire group's role, to make explicit who is giving this group its assignments, and to describe the responsibilities of individual members. This statement provides an important tool for recruiting and orienting new members and for monitoring the performance of the group. This statement can be revised as the purpose and structure of the group evolve. If it is a temporary group, the statement should note when it will dissolve.

A statement of organization and purpose should address the following items:

♦ Explicit statement of why the advisory group exists;

♦ Description of the selection process and to whom the advisory group reports;

♦ Length of term of service and duration of the committee;

♦ Job description that identifies the specific responsibilities or expectations of individual members;

♦ Titles and duties of officers;

♦ Number of meetings;

♦ Criteria for membership;

♦ Relationship of advisory group to governing or statutory board; and

♦ Relationship of the staff to the advisory group.

Appendix C includes a sample statement of organization and purpose for an advisory committee established for fund-raising purposes.

A well-formulated statement of organization and purpose and a job description for individual members will not transform a mediocre advisory group into a strong one, but it is hard to imagine an advisory committee succeeding without them. Because purpose and structure may be altered in the course of the advisory committee's life, these statements will be reviewed and revised as the committee grows and changes. Annual review of this statement also provides the committee, staff, and governing board with an opportunity to clarify their respective roles and to review the committee's performance.

V. CASE #3: The Attitude and Expectations of the Executive Director

Tim Larue has been manager of public radio station WONT for three years. The governing board of the state university that holds the license for WONT requires that Tim and his staff work with an advisory committee composed of community leaders who are selected by the university board (which votes on candidates submitted by members of the staff and the committee). Tim's tireless efforts to build the station's staff, audience, and budget have been successful. He has always resented having to take time away from his considerable day-to-day management responsibilities to "schmooze with a bunch of folks who haven't done beans for this station."

The most crucial ingredient for building a successful advisory committee is the quality of staff leadership. The executive director or a senior administrator is typically the linchpin in this relationship. How much help should the executive director be prepared to give the advisory committee? Unfortunately, it is simply not realistic to expect most advisory committees to staff themselves. If the executive director is not willing to devote or assign staff time to orienting, educating, motivating committee members and helping them carry out their responsibilities, the busy professionals and volunteers who serve on the advisory committee are unlikely to make much progress on their own.

In Tim's case, because the advisory board was created by a higher authority, he does not have the luxury of determining whether or not it should continue to exist. (In some cases, the advisory board may not even have direct contact with an existing governing board. For example, some public radio stations that are university licensees report to a university department head.) On the other hand, Tim might be wasting a good opportunity to use this group to build community support for the station. Because the university board has been receptive to nominations from others to fill advisory committee vacancies, Tim and his staff might want to spend more time identifying the kinds of people they think are most likely to be helpful as advisory board members.

Tim's attitude is undoubtedly influenced by the fact that he feels overworked and understaffed. It may also be a function of other experiences and attitudes about advisory groups that he brings with him from past jobs with nonprofit organizations. For example, one of the dangers of activating Tim's advisory committee to play a stronger role in positioning the station in the community may be to encourage it to interfere with decisions about the station's programming. A related issue is the case of the successful advisory committee that begins to perceive itself as a decision-making group, thereby vesting itself with more authority than it actually has.

The executive director can minimize the risk of intrusive committee members by clarifying the role of committee members (as well as the staff who work with them) as much as possible. Advisory committee members will better accept the impropriety of intruding into the management domain if they understand the matters over which the advisory committee does *not* have management authority or jurisdiction. Advisory committee members can be educated about their role through: an orientation for new members when they join the committee; the opportunity to observe mentors on the committee who understand the different roles of the staff, the governing board, and the advisory committee; and regular opportunities for continuing education on how program decisions are made.

Those who work with advisory committees must find a balance between overwhelming the committee members and boring them! Furthermore, because advisory committees are both human and democratic enterprises, senior staff and committee leaders must expect some disagreement and conflict (and hopefully a healthy dose of creative tension) from time to time.

VI. CASE #4: A Systematic Selection and Orientation Process

The advisory committee for the Little Valley Shelter for the Homeless has always filled vacancies casually by periodically asking current committee members to identify friends who might be willing to serve. Many members of the staff and the advisory committee anticipate a growing need for this group to establish links with key, potentially supportive organizations in the surrounding community. The executive director keeps reminding the committee of the need for new kinds of skills and agency affiliations on the committee. Most members agree wholeheartedly, and they are also becoming increasingly frustrated with the agency's inability to attract more prominent members of the community to committee service.

This committee has two problems: deciding who it wants and recruiting them to serve. A thoughtful, systematic process of identifying and selecting the kinds of people who are desirable members of the advisory group is critical in building a successful advisory committee. The following tools can enhance the selection process for those advisory committees that will be around for some time. For those that are more temporary, this investment in time may not be warranted.

A. A nominating subcommittee or group composed of the most able and influential leaders of the advisory committee and the organization it serves. The executive director should be a member.

B. A formal job description for the committee and a statement of the responsibilities (see example in Appendix C) to be used in recruitment and orientation.

C. A written profile that identifies the ideal composition of the committee and compares current composition against that ideal (e.g., the knowledge, skills, and experience of the individual members). A committee profile also helps the group to build pluralism and diversity into its membership.

D. A plan for reaching out to other constituencies that can help the nominating group identify prospects to fill the membership needs of the committee (e.g., inviting suggestions from other members of the existing committee, the governing board, the staff, and other publics such as funders or community leaders).

E. A process for cultivating prospective new members to educate them about their role and to increase the chances of their willingness to serve.

F. A thoughtful strategy for inviting new members to serve (such as a personal visit from the advisory committee chair or the executive director).

G. An orientation program for new members that sets the stage for them to learn about the mission and values of the organization and the role of the advisory committee.

H. Helping new committee members to feel part of the organization as soon as possible.

It is not unusual for an external group or official (such as a local government authority) to retain the authority to select the members of the advisory committee. Nor is it unusual for the executive director to control the selection process. The most desirable model will provide the appointing authority with sufficient input from the advisory committee's members, the executive director, staff members, and other individuals and groups who are in a position to identify qualified candidates.

The quality and commitment of those selected to serve on the committee will influence its effectiveness. Advisory groups that are authorized to fill their own vacancies should take advantage of this power to strengthen their membership. Those that do not have the authority must develop creative ways to influence the selection authority. They can, for example, provide the "selectors" with names of candidates or with criteria that describe the qualifications of the ideal candidate.

VII. CASE #5: The Relationship Between the Statutory Body and the Advisory Committee

The Development Advisory Council of the Association of Local Health Officers (ALHO) was established to help raise money for the association. The corporate managers, professional development officers, and private hospital administrators who serve on this council have added visibility and support to the association. Recently, the Development Advisory Council scored a big win by raising foundation and corporation funds to finance a major new program to educate the public on preventive efforts for good health. After three years of service, many of the professional development officers who serve on this advisory council are starting to burn out. One member asks at a recent council meeting, "If we are doing such a great job, why aren't we being asked to serve on the governing board?"

As a practical matter, individuals on ALHO's Development Advisory Council may neither be eligible nor qualified to serve on the governing board. If the members of the ALHO advisory council are not professional local health officers or members of the association, they may not be eligible for membership on the governing board. The association can continue this policy or revise it so that at-large members are eligible for governing board service. If they are eligible, some of the council members may make excellent candidates for governing board service. Like those who serve in a capital campaign, members of an advisory committee can be cultivated to become more seriously involved with the organization by eventually becoming members of the governing board.

Other factors are also important. ALHO needs to consider whether it is keeping council members on too long or overworking them. Part of the underlying problem may also be related to the lack of recognition from the governing board of ALHO. The executive director of ALHO and her Vice President for Development should not be the only people working with and supporting the advisory council. The governing board should acknowledge the advisory council's importance to the organization.

How can a governing board build a productive relationship with an advisory committee? Here are some ways.

A. Invite the chairperson of the advisory committee to serve as a voting or non-voting member of the governing board or on a committee of the board.

B. Invite the chairperson of the advisory committee to make regular reports at governing board meetings.

C. Invite members of the advisory committee to attend portions of individual board meetings, or plan social activities that allow members of both groups to meet informally.

D. Formally recognize members whose terms of service come to an end (see Case #8).

VIII. CASE #6: The Continuing Education of the Advisory Committee

Two of the most prominent members of public television station WRST's Community Advisory Committee recently resigned before the end of their first term. While they both claim the press of other commitments as the primary reason, one of the departing members, Paul Gonzales, confides to the committee chairperson that both he and his colleague are disillusioned with their experience as advisory committee members. Specifically, Gonzales observes that he agreed to serve with high hopes for becoming a productive member and contributing to the station's public affairs campaign devoted to celebrating cultural diversity. However, he still does not understand what the station is all about and what was expected of him individually. He had been excited about the prospect of applying his experience as a successful marketing executive to the station, but he saw no real opportunity to contribute. Furthermore, Gonzales suspects that the community advisory committee was established merely to fulfill a requirement by the university licensee for this station.

Although no precise formula determines the amount of time to put into advisory committee development, the care and feeding of an advisory group can be a major investment. Furthermore, it is an ongoing process that must be established and maintained, rather than a single event that will produce transformation. Too many nonprofits that want to establish advisory groups overlook the staff time and expenses required to inform and educate this group.

The Community Advisory Committee for WRST may be suffering from problems that are more fundamental than lack of education. Nevertheless, it appears that the station – its governing board and executive director – have paid little attention to orientating and educating the committee on the work of the station, the role of the committee, and the responsibilities of individual committee members.

New committee members as well as more experienced ones need regular assistance in learning about the needs and accomplishments of the station, and in deciphering their own role. Activities that contribute to the continuing education of the committee include:

A. Inviting key staff or governing board members to make reports at advisory committee meetings that address the mission, vision, and activities of the organization.

B. Enabling committee members to observe the way the organization works by experiencing its programs and services firsthand.

C. Managing a reasonable flow of information between meetings that keeps the advisory committee informed of key activities. This flow might include a special newsletter, a regular memo from the executive director, or copies of existing reports that are relevant to the work of the advisory group. The staff who prepares this information must be able to choose the highly relevant from the marginal.

D. Planning a retreat or special committee meeting to give the advisors an opportunity to review their responsibilities, identify priorities to strengthen their performance, and get to know each other better.

E. Inviting members of the advisory committee to social events that allow them to meet informally with representatives of the organization's publics.

IX. CASE #7: The Organization of the Committee

The Advisory Committee for the Transylvania Symphony Orchestra (TSO) includes 32 people who have been asked to help achieve a critical objective—to help the board of directors and staff expand and diversify the subscriber base for the annual concert series. Attendance at recent advisory committee meetings has waned. The meetings start late and end late. The committee president, the managing director, and the music director have doled out plenty of assignments but they can't seem to get the advisory committee to do anything except socialize with each other at these meetings.

The effectiveness of an advisory committee will be influenced by the structure of its organization and the conduct of its meetings. The larger the advisory group, the more formal should be the division of labor among its members. A committee of TSO's size should form subcommittees charged with key tasks to help it carry out its mission. TSO may also decide to reduce the size of its advisory committee. Advisory groups with fewer than 10 members are unlikely to need committees, but it still helps to assign specific tasks to individual members.

What other organizational factors are likely to strengthen an advisory group? Here are some examples.

A. A strong, knowledgeable chairperson of the advisory committee who understands the purpose of the group, is committed to giving more time than others, and is skilled at conducting meetings. Ideally, the person who serves as vice chairperson is the most likely successor to the current chairperson.

B. A rotation plan for committee membership and officers. A limit on the total number of terms each committee member can serve is the best way for most committees to continue to add qualified new members. In the absence of limited terms, an advisory committee must depend more on an assessment process to determine whether individual committee members should be invited to complete a second and subsequent terms. Because formal evaluation of individual committee members is rarely done in advisory committees, the practice of unlimited terms often results in allowing individual committee members to remain on the committee indefinitely.

C. Not all advisory committees require consensus on recommendations or even the need to meet formally. Where required, meetings should be more than ceremonial. Effective meetings are a result of a well-developed agenda, adequate supporting materials sent to committee members before the meeting, and a skilled chairperson. The number of meetings will depend on the role of the group.

X. CASE #8: Recognizing Committee Service

After two years of attending biannual advisory committee meetings for an innovative, interdisciplinary program developed at a nonprofit hospital, Ann Jones stops receiving information. When she inquires about the status of the group, she learns that the program still exists but that the advisory committee has been discontinued due to lack of funds.

Obviously, members should be notified of changes in the status of the advisory committee. Unfortunately, it is quite common for advisory groups to be created with great fanfare, and then dissipated or quietly discontinued altogether. Even a weak or inactive committee deserves to be informed of its demise.

Even more common is the practice of allowing individual committee members to complete their term of service without recognition. Like members of governing boards, members of advisory committees tend to be busy people who are donating precious time from their jobs, their families, and other voluntary activities to contribute in this manner. Their work should be recognized from time to time, both during their term of service and when they complete their term.

Methods of recognition should be suited to the culture (as well as the budget) of the organization. Recognition practices include:

♦ Special recognition plaque or gift;

♦ Formal presentation at the committee member's last meeting;

♦ Letter of thanks signed by the chairperson and chief staff officer;

♦ Special ceremony (e.g., luncheon, dinner, reception); and

♦ Acknowledging service through the organization's newsletter.

Some advisory committees are terminated altogether because the organization they serve makes the transition to independent status, with a governing board superceding the advisory committee. Even though the individual members may well be prepared for this transition, each should be formally thanked individually for his or her service.

XI. CONCLUSION

Advisory committees can make a real difference to the nonprofit sector, yet they often suffer from an ambiguous status. Nonprofit organizations sense their potential to help the staff and governing board do wondrous things, but are often ambivalent about what they really want advisory groups to accomplish, or how they can help them do it.

Effective advisory committees do not form themselves. The art of creating successful advisory committees has been mastered by some and abandoned by others who choose not to invest the time and resources into building such a group once it is established. Others never learn it at all, waiting in vain for the advisory committee to "work better."

An advisory committee's reason for existence should be real, legitimate, and important. When a compelling case for its purpose can be buttressed by the commitment to invest the necessary resources into engaging such a group, it is worth doing, and worth doing well.

APPENDIX A

Deciding Whether to Create (or Renew) an Advisory Committee: Questions to Consider in Advance

1. What is the purpose of the committee:
   ◆ What does the agency want it to accomplish?
   ◆ What role will it play in the organization?

2. What will the organization expect the individual members of the committee to do to achieve the above purpose?

3. To whom will this committee report?

4. Who will have the authority to select its members?

5. Who will provide the staff support to orient, educate, and work with the members of the committee?
   ◆ How much time will this take?
   ◆ Whose responsibility is it?

6. How will the organization recruit members of the group?

7. How large should the committee be to carry out its purpose?
   ◆ Will it need subcommittees?

8. What is the nature of the relationship between the governing board, the staff, and the advisory committee?

9. What are the financial costs for the committee on an annual basis (e.g. travel, meals, materials, staff support)?

10. To what extent are the executive director and the officers of the governing board in favor of the committee?

11. Will the committee members need liability insurance?

APPENDIX B

Common Problems with Advisory Committees

1. Lack of clarity in purpose, role, or scope.

2. Ignorance about or lack of commitment to mission of parent organization.

3. Unclear expectations of individual members.

4. Lack of leadership and support from the executive director or other key staff members.

5. Improper or inappropriate composition.

6. Weak organization and structure.

7. Lack of interaction with and feedback from the governing board or appointing authority.

8. Under-utilizing of advisory board members.

9. Overstepping advisory role.

10. Absence of orientation and/or continuing education programs.

11. Haphazard selection process.

12. Formed to "fix" an organization in crisis.

APPENDIX C

Statement of Organization
and
Purpose for the Advisory Committee
of Agency XYZ

PURPOSE

To help the board of directors and executive director of Agency XYZ in the solicitation of gifts and grants from individuals, corporations, and foundations.

MEMBERSHIP

The number of members of the advisory committee shall be no more than twenty. The executive director and board chairperson of XYZ shall serve as members of the advisory committee.

SELECTION

During the initial year, members should be elected by the board of directors and, thereafter, by the established membership of the advisory committee.

TERM OF OFFICE

An advisory committee member serves a three-year term. To enable new people to join, a member can be elected to a maximum of two consecutive three-year terms, but then must be off the committee for at least one year before being eligible for an additional one or two terms. To ensure continuity in the committee's work, terms will be staggered, requiring that on the initial committee one-third of the members will serve one-year terms, one-third will serve two-year terms, and one-third will serve three-year terms. One- and two-year terms will not be counted in limiting consecutive committee service to two three-year terms.

MEMBER RESPONSIBILITIES

Each committee member is expected to:

1) Attend a minimum of two meetings per year.
2) Actively participate in the functioning of the committee.
3) Be available for individual consultation to the executive director.

4) Occasionally accompany a director, officer, or staff of XYZ for personal solicitation of selected prospects.

5) Write or sign letters endorsing XYZ's solicitations.

OFFICERS

1) A chairperson, a vice chairperson, and a secretary shall be the officers of the advisory committee.

2) The chairperson shall be invited to attend all regular meetings of the board of directors.

3) The chairperson shall preside at all meetings of the advisory committee.

STAFF SUPPORT

The executive director of the XYZ shall act as executive secretary to the committee.

SUGGESTED RESOURCES

Axelrod, Nancy R. *The Chief Executive's Role in Developing the Nonprofit Board.* Washington, D.C.: National Center for Nonprofit Boards, 1988, 22 pages.

This booklet identifies eight ways the chief staff officer can strengthen the governing board so that both the board and chief executive work effectively to fulfill the organization's mission. The booklet includes a practical grid to help identify and select new board members.

Howe, Fisher. *The Board Member's Guide to Fund Raising: What Every Trustee Needs to Know about Raising Money.* San Francisco, CA: Jossey-Bass Publisher, Inc., 1991, 168 pages. (Available from the National Center for Nonprofit Boards.)

This book, with a foreword by David Rockefeller, highlights the need for board understanding and responsibility in fund raising. Key specific elements of a successful fund raising program are featured, with discussion encouraging and motivating active board member participation. The book covers the entire fund raising process, and shows board members how they can be effective in fulfilling this aspect of their role.

Ingram, Richard T. *Making Advisory Committees and Boards Work.* Washington, D.C.: Association of Governing Boards of Universities and Colleges, 1989, 19 pages.

This pamphlet addresses the function of college and university advisory committees and offers approaches for how to utilize them more effectively.

Mueller, Robert K. *The Director's and Officer's Guide to Advisory Boards.* Westport, CT: Greenwood Press, 1990, 277 pages.

Written primarily for corporate directors and officers, this book deals with the advisory board in the corporate environment. Discussion includes the functions of advisory boards and statutory boards; basic differences between advisory boards and statutory boards; and guidelines for making the most effective use of these advisory bodies in managing corporations.

Nelson, Judith Grummon. *Six Keys to Recruiting, Orienting, and Involving Nonprofit Board Members.* Washington, D.C.: National Center for Nonprofit Boards, 1991, 58 pages.

This handbook provides a step-by-step approach to help organizations and nominating committees maintain active governing boards by attracting qualified and committed new members. Discussion features assessing board needs, identifying and cultivating prospects, and recruiting and involving new members. Detailed suggestions, model forms, sample letters, and checklists are supplied.

Tremper, Charles and George Babcock. *The Nonprofit Board's Role in Risk Management: More Than Buying Insurance.* Washington, D.C.: National Center for Nonprofit Boards, 1990, 20 pages.

This booklet demystifies the fundamentals of risk management and the board's critical role in understanding and controlling the wide range of common—yet oftentimes hidden—risks that are inherent in all organizations. It describes both the need for, and the shortcomings of, liability insurance and other coverage in instances such as property damage, personal injury, and employee grievances.

ABOUT THE AUTHOR

Nancy R. Axelrod is executive director of the National Center for Nonprofit Boards. Prior to her appointment as NCNB's founding executive, she served as vice president for programs and public policy for the Association of Governing Boards of Universities and Colleges, where she designed and conducted educational programs for college and university trustees. Ms. Axelrod has served as a board member, staff member, and board development consultant to numerous advisory and governing boards. She has written on nonprofit trusteeship, governance, and board-staff relations, and has served as a speaker at many conferences and workshops devoted to these topics.